Contents

Published by Diabetes UK **Food photography** Bill Reavell
Design Paul Grimes and Emma Blacker **Recipes developed by** Louise Tyler

What is diabetes?

Diabetes mellitus is a condition in which the amount of glucose (sugar) in the blood is too high because the body cannot use it properly. Glucose comes from the digestion of starchy foods such as bread, rice, potatoes, chapatis, yams and plantain, from sugar and other sweet foods, and from the liver which makes glucose.

Insulin is vital for life. It is a hormone produced by the pancreas, which helps the glucose to enter the cells where it is used as fuel by the body.

The main symptoms of untreated diabetes are increased thirst, going to the loo all the time – especially at night, extreme tiredness, weight loss, genital itching or regular episodes of thrush, and blurred vision.

Type 1 (insulin dependent) diabetes develops if the body is unable to produce any insulin. This type of diabetes usually appears before the age of 40. It is treated by insulin injections and diet.

Type 2 (non insulin dependent) diabetes develops when the body can still make some insulin, but not enough, or when the insulin that is produced does not work properly (known as insulin resistance). This type of diabetes usually appears in people over the age of 40, though often appears before the age of 40 in South Asian and African-Caribbean people. It is treated by diet alone or by diet and tablets or, sometimes, by diet and insulin injections.

The main aim of treatment of both types of diabetes is to achieve near normal blood glucose and blood pressure levels. This, together with a healthy lifestyle, will help to improve wellbeing and protect against long-term damage to the eyes, kidneys, nerves, heart and major arteries.

Part one

Introduction

Home baked foods including cakes and biscuits are one of life's real pleasures – a slice of moist chocolate cake, a crumbly biscuit or fresh bread warm from the oven. Many people with diabetes think that they must steer clear of certain foods, but this is not so. Although cakes and biscuits should be limited as part of balanced eating, you do need to cut them out completely.

Good blood glucose control can still be achieved when sugar and foods containing sugar are eaten. Dietary management of diabetes depends on basing meals on starchy carbohydrate foods like bread and pasta and including more fruit, vegetables and pulses in your everyday diet.

Foods like cakes and biscuits should not be forming a regular part of your daily diet, particularly if you are overweight, but should be kept to special occasions.

This book aims to show you that you can still enjoy baking and, with just a little guidance, recipes can be adapted and made more suitable for people with diabetes.

Even if you are a complete beginner this book will lead you through the basics of home baking so you can create delicious and impressive bakes you never thought possible!

Six steps to eating a healthy diet

1 Eat regular meals based on starchy foods such as bread, pasta, chapatis, potatoes, rice and cereals. This will help you to control blood glucose levels.

2 Try to cut down on the fat you eat, particularly saturated fats as this type of fat is linked to heart disease. Eating less fat and fatty foods will also help you to lose weight.

3 Eat more fruit and vegetables – aim for at least five portions a day to provide you with vitamins and fibre as well as helping to balance your overall diet.

4 Cut down on sugar and sugary foods. This does not mean you need to try to eat a sugar free diet. Sugar can be used as an ingredient in foods and in baking as part of a healthy diet.

5 Use less salt. Try flavouring foods with herbs and spices rather than adding salt to food.

6 Drink alcohol in moderation only – that's 2 units of alcohol per day for a woman (2 glasses of wine) and 3 units per day for a man (1½ pints ordinary strength beer or lager). Remember never to drink on an empty stomach as alcohol can make hypoglycaemia (low blood glucose levels) more likely to occur.

Diabetic foods

Diabetes UK does not recommend the use of specially formulated 'diabetic' cakes and biscuits. There is no evidence to suggest that these products offer any special advantages to people with diabetes.

The most important concern is that the term 'diabetic' attached to a food may make people with diabetes, their relatives, friends or carers think that they can be eaten freely and can even be therapeutically beneficial.

Diabetic foods are simply a range of confectionery, cakes, biscuits and jams which are sweetened with nutritive sweetening agents like sorbitol and fructose rather than ordinary sucrose.

Nowadays, as far as sugar content is concerned, ordinary cakes and biscuits can be eaten as part of a balanced diet without being detrimental to diabetes control. However, they are usually high in fat and therefore calories.

Using diabetic foods encourages the myth that the diet for people with diabetes is a special one and goes against healthy eating advice for people with diabetes which focuses on balancing food choices and keeping to a healthy weight.

Baking and balanced eating

Over the last few years there has been a rapid growth in the availability of reduced fat, reduced sugar and high fibre foods.

Such foods can make a valuable contribution to a healthy diet when eaten regularly and in large amounts. For example, choosing a low fat milk over full fat milk on a daily basis will make a beneficial reduction to your total fat intake.

Cakes and biscuits do not form a large part of a balanced diet. If you only eat cakes and biscuits occasionally, eating low fat or low sugar versions will not make a big difference to your everyday diet. However, if you eat cakes and biscuits more regularly, reduced fat or sugar varieties will only be helpful if they are eaten in no greater quantitiy than you would ordinary or standard cakes and biscuits .

Glycaemic index

The glycaemic index (GI) is a ranking of individual foods according to the effect they have on blood glucose levels. Carbohydrate foods with a low GI cause a slow steady rise in blood glucose levels.

High GI foods cause blood glucose levels to rise quickly – this is because they are digested and absorbed more rapidly. For example the GI of glucose is 100 whereas the GI of baked beans is 48. Even though you may not have heard the term GI before, you may already have been encouraged to include low GI foods such as pasta and pulses in your diet.

You can't tell a low GI food just by looking at it – and GI is not just related to the fibre or sugar content of a food. The effect of a meal or snack on blood glucose levels is influenced by many things. For example, the way in which a food is cooked and prepared, the combination of foods you eat with it and their fat and protein content as well as other foods you have eaten that day, can all have a bearing on its GI.

There is more to eating a healthy diet than just eating low GI foods. A food is not good or bad because of its GI. It is neither necessary, nor practical to look at specific GI values for every food you eat. However, including more low GI foods in your meals can help to improve blood glucose control and will help curb your appetite by making you feel fuller for longer, so you are less likely to overeat.

Low GI foods for baking

Fruit dried or fresh, used as fillings and toppings

Wholegrains barley, bulgar wheat, Basmati rice, plain popcorn, oatmeal

Breakfast cereals porridge, Allbran, muesli

Dairy milk, yogurt

Breads pumpernickel or rye bread, pitta bread, fruit loaf

Snacks

People with diabetes are advised to spread their food intake evenly across the day by eating regular meals and also having a snack in between meals. Snacks may not be essential, particularly if you are trying to lose weight, but it may be necessary to include snacks in your routine diet if you are treated with insulin.

Children and people who are very active are likely to need extra energy from snacks between meals. This is to minimise the risk of hypoglycaemia and to help to promote good blood glucose control.

Having snacks does not necessarily mean eating more calories in your daily diet. The idea is to spread your food intake out more evenly. If you are trying to lose weight, choose fruit instead of cakes and biscuits.

Part two

Adapting recipes

The recipes in this book have all been adapted as far as possible, to be lower in fat, and have a reduced amount of sugar. Some use wholemeal flour or a mixture of wholemeal and white to increase the fibre content of the recipe.

Other ingredients may also be used, for instance porridge oats or oatmeal, to increase the soluble fibre which helps to lower blood glucose fats like cholesterol and helps promote good blood glucose control. You can add fruit or even vegetables, for instance grated carrot or courgette, into a cake mix to add fibre and flavour – as well as essential vitamins and minerals.

- Try to replace butter with a mono or polyunsaturated fat, or try and use a reduced fat spread where possible or use a fat replacement, see page 10.

- When filling cakes try to use lower fat alternatives to whipped double cream or butter cream. For instance, you can use a mixture of whipped whipping cream and yogurt, or light crème fraîche with fresh fruit. See the box on page 11.

- Try to reduce the amount of sugar or replace some sugar with dried fruit. This will help provide sweetness and also give extra fibre and minerals, such as iron.

- Replace some of the white flour in the recipe with wholemeal – up to a half will give good results, but more than this can give a heavy result. For plainer cakes such as Victoria sandwich or Madeira, keep to white flour as this gives the best results.

Fats in baking

One of the most important factors about adapting recipes when you have diabetes is the amount and type of fat that you use. Most of the recipes in this book will use margarine or spreads. In some cases butter is used where the flavour and end result is better than when using margarine.

Use margarines or spreads, which are based on monounsaturated fats **(MUFA)**, such as olive and rapeseed based spreads or polyunsaturated fats **(PUFA)**, which are based on sunflower, safflower, corn and soya oils. It is particularly important to eat less saturated animal fat. A diet high in this type of fat is linked to heart disease – and if you have diabetes you are already at greater risk of developing heart disease.

Fats in baking				
Product	**Total fat per 100g**	**saturated fat**	**PUFA**	**MUFA**
Butter	81.7g	54.8g	2.7g	20g
Low fat spread	40g	26.8g	1.2g	20g
Very low fat spread*	23.8g	6.2g	4.8g	11.9g
Hard margarine	79.3g	34.6g	5.4g	36.2g
MUFA spread – reduced fat	59g	14g	14g	32g
Rapeseed oil	99.9g	6.6g	29.3g	59.3g
Sunflower oil	99.9g	12g	63.3g	20.5g
PUFA margarine	82.8g	17g	36g	26.6g

Because of their high water and low fat content these are not suitable for cooking

Fillings and toppings for cakes

Whip 150ml/^{1}/$_4$ pint whipping cream until it forms soft peaks, fold through1 chopped mango, and the flesh of 2 passion fruits then beat a little more if necessary

Beat 1 x 200g carton light cream cheese with 2 tablespoons icing sugar and the grated rind 1 lemon, lime or orange

Whip 150ml/^{1}/$_4$ pint whipping cream with 1 tablespoon icing sugar then fold through 75g/2^3/$_4$oz halved blueberries and 1 tablespoon chopped fresh mint

Mix together 50g/1^3/$_4$oz puréed apple, 1 x 200g carton of reduced fat cream cheese and a pinch cinnamon.

For almond paste and icing recipes see also page 70

Replacing saturated fats with mono or polyunsaturated fats can help to lower blood fats like cholesterol, which in turn is beneficial in helping to reduce the risk of heart disease.

Oil can be used in place of fat in some recipes. There is a range of oils available so choose those which are high in MUFA or PUFA. However oil is still 100 per cent fat.

Note: Reducing the amount of fat, reduced fat spreads or low fat spreads used in many recipes may reduce the 'storage time' of the cake or biscuit.

Replacing fat

In some recipes it is possible to cut out the fat completely or replace the fat with an alternative. The method used in preparation, ie 'whisking', 'rubbing in', 'creaming', 'all-in-one' can make a difference to the choice and amount of fat used, and the end result that you require, eg a dark heavy texture and appearance or a light pale one.

Low fat methods

Cake recipes using the whisking method require no added fat, for example the chocolate roulade on page 12.

A date purée is made to replace the fat in the chocolate brownies on page 40. Why not make your own date purée and use it in some of your own recipes? 100g/3½oz purée will replace 200g/7oz fat. The purée would not be suited to cakes with a pale appearance.

Date purée

Place 175g/6oz chopped stoned dried dates into a pan with 100ml/3½fl oz water and simmer for 2–3 minutes until the dates are soft. Leave to cool.

Prune purée which acts in the same way as date purée is available ready made in jars from most supermarkets.

Sugar in baking

There are a number of reasons why sugar is used in baking. Probably the most obvious are that of taste and texture. But sugar also plays a very important part in the science behind baking. It provides recipes with bulk, ie allowing air to be incorporated and held in the mixture. It also helps act as a preservative for the finished result.

Although the amount of sugar in traditional baking recipes is the amount needed to give the best results, the sugar in recipes can generally be reduced by up to a half with good end results.

The recipes in this book have been made using a reduced amount of sugar, be it caster, demerara or liquid sugars like honey and syrup.

However they will tend to be a little drier and will not keep as long as a traditional recipe. So, where suitable, you could freeze in portions and defrost as necessary. All the recipes in this book are indicated as to whether or not they are suitable for freezing.

Different types of sugar are used simply for a matter of taste, texture and appearance, but all sugars affect blood glucose levels and have a similar nutritional composition. The sugar in recipes can be further reduced when adding dried fruits, eg apricots or sultanas. This will also add some essential vitamins and minerals.

Fructose (fruit sugar) used to be recommended for baking for people with diabetes. However, it is not as superior as ordinary sugar in baking and does not provide any particular benefit for people with diabetes. It still contains the same amount of calories as ordinary sugar and also raises blood glucose levels.

Even though a cake may contain what seems like a large amount of sugar, in reality you will only be having a small portion of the total recipe and therefore a relatively small amount of sugar.

Diabetes UK does not recommend the use of artificial/intense sweeteners in baking. There is no real substitute for ordinary sugar when it comes to baking as intense sweeteners do not provide the bulk required, so the end result can be flat and heavy. They also tend to turn bitter on heating.

Part three

Basic baking ingredients

In this chapter are explanations of basic baking ingredients and how they can be used. You can vary the ingredients to get the results you want. For example you can use different dried fruits or flours or add ingredients such as oats.

Flours For cakes, self-raising white flour is usually used. A half and half mixture of wholemeal and white flour also works. The end result is just a bit heavier and darker.

Using all wholemeal flour in cakes results in a much heavier, more solid cake which can be an ideal texture for a fruit loaf. When using all wholemeal flour, the mixture may require more liquid.

There are a number of different flours on the shelves and they are generally classified by their extraction rate:

Wholemeal or wholewheat are 100% extraction where nothing is taken away. The outer husk of the wheat grain and the wheatgerm of the grain is included in the flour giving it its nutty flavour and texture, and making it high in fibre.

Brown or wheatmeal are usually 85–90% extraction as the outer husk of the wheat grain has been removed but the wheatgerm is still present. Brown bread has a lighter texture than wholemeal bread but is lower in fibre.

White is usually 72–74% extraction rate, with all of the outer husk of the wheatgrain, bran and wheatgerm removed, making it low in fibre.

Strong plain is used for most bread making as it has a high gluten content, enabling a good rise and allowing air to become trapped to give a light airy texture.

Gluten free – if you have coeliac disease or you are baking for someone with the condition you must use a gluten free flour such as rice flour or cornflour, available on prescription or from your pharmacy/health food shop and some supermarkets.

It really is a case of trial and error when substituting for 'normal' flour. Recipes are generally found on the pack of gluten free flours or in a leaflet from the manufacturers, for you to follow, so it is usually best to stick to these as they have been tried and tested.

Oats These flattened flakes of grain are sometimes added to cakes, biscuits and other home bakes. They provide a good source of fibre and some vitamins and minerals. Oats have a low GI making them a good addition to home bakes. Try adding them to your own recipes.

Sugar There are many types of sugar available in the shops, different ones suited to different types of cooking or recipes.

Caster sugar is best for whisked and creamed cakes because the fine crystals dissolve and blend quickly with other ingredients.

Granulated sugar is mostly used for syrups or for cakes that require a slightly coarser texture.

Icing sugar should be sieved before use. It is best used for icing and fillings, and in some pastries and biscuits. It is not suitable for cakes as it does not provide enough bulk to the mixture, resulting in a rather dense thin cake.

Light and dark muscavado/soft sugar provide a good colour, a moist textured cake and a delicious caramel flavour.

Demerara has a delicious texture and slight caramel flavour give a great addition to fruit and spiced cakes.

Golden syrup or honey give a good flavour and moist texture to cakes, but is used in addition to sugar or replacing a portion of the sugar, as honey or syrup alone will not provide enough bulk to the mixture.

Dried fruit A great way of adding extra fibre to home bakes, they can also enable you to cut down on some of the sugar used in baking as they will provide extra sweetness. Dried fruits are also a source of some vitamins and minerals.

Yeast So easy now with easy blend dried yeast so readily available. You can still use fresh yeast which you may get from health food shops or bakers, but for ease and speed opt for the dried versions.

Fats For cake making, fat should be used at room temperature to ensure easy and even distribution. Some recipes such as pastry may require cold fat to give a better result.

Butter can be used in recipes for special occasions but polyunsaturated or monounsaturated margarines can be used instead, with very good results. Some recipes work well using a reduced fat spread, but it can be a case of trial and error. The fat in recipes can be replaced by a date purée. This however only really suits a darker cake mixture.

Eggs These should be stored at room temperature for at least an hour before starting to bake. In these recipes large eggs are used, unless specified otherwise.

Young people, old people, pregnant women and anyone with an immune deficiency disease should avoid eating raw or lightly cooked eggs which may cause salmonella.

Part four

Recipes

Bread

baking

Bread is a staple part of our diets and is a good source of starchy carbohydrate for people with diabetes.

Although most commonly eaten at breakfast or with afternoon tea, it can help balance meals throughout the day, accompanying soups, salads, pasta or rice dishes.

Baking bread can be quite a long process involving different stages as follows.

Kneading This may seem time consuming but is absolutely necessary as a means of giving a good texture and evenly distributing the gases produced by the yeast. Place the dough onto a lightly floured work surface. Fold the dough in half towards you then stretch it away from you using the heel of your hand. Give the dough a quarter of a turn and repeat a folding-pushing-rocking motion. Continue until the dough is smooth, elastic and is no longer sticky.

Rising

After kneading, the dough is left to rise until doubled in size. Place the dough in a lightly oiled bowl, cover with a damp cloth or clingfilm and set aside – leaving the bowl in a warm place will aid the process.

Knocking back and proving

Punch all the air out of the dough with your fist, or re-knead for a couple of minutes. Shape then leave to prove (rise) in the prepared tin before baking, allowing the mixture to become light and airy.

Cooking times

When varying ingredients are used, it can be harder to gauge the timing. The best way to test whether the loaf is cooked is to remove from the tin and tap the bottom. A hollow sound will signify that is cooked. If not, return to the oven out of the tin and cook for a few more minutes.

Simple white loaf

Preparation and cooking time 1½−2 hours
Serves 12 • Suitable for freezing

600g/1lb 5oz strong white flour

25g/1oz butter at room temperature

1 x 7g sachet easy blend dried yeast

1 teaspoon salt

pinch sugar

400ml/14floz warm milk

a little extra flour for kneading

Preheat the oven to 200°C/400°F/gas mark 6.

Rub together the flour and butter, until the mixture resembles fine breadcrumbs. Stir in the yeast, salt and the sugar. Make a well in the centre of the dough and pour in the milk. Mix together to form a soft dough (it is easiest to do this with your hands). If the dough seems a little sticky then add a little extra flour; if it is too dry then add a little extra liquid.

Tip the dough out onto a lightly floured surface and knead for 8−10 minutes until smooth and elastic. Place the dough in a lightly oiled bowl, cover with a damp cloth and set aside until doubled in size. Tip out onto a lightly floured surface and knock back. The dough can either be shaped and place into a 900g/2lb loaf tin or divide the dough into 12 pieces, shape each into a roll. Place the rolls into a 23cm deep cake tin. Or divide the dough into three, roll into ropes and plait, or simply shape into rolls and place on a baking sheet. Cover and leave to prove for 30 minutes then bake for about 30 minutes until golden and hollow when tapped on the bottom.

Cool slightly before serving. Or cool and store in a bread bin or paper bag.

Variation: Add 5 chopped sun-dried tomatoes and 1 tablespoon fresh chopped thyme or 100g/3½ oz chopped ready-to-eat dried apricots and 75g/2¾ oz toasted sunflower seeds by kneading through the dough after its first rising.

PER SERVING			
energy	protein	carbohydrate	fat
207 kcal	**7** grams	**40** grams	**4** grams

Wholemeal loaf

Preparation and cooking time 1½–2 hours
Serves 12 • Suitable for freezing

600g/1lb 5oz wholewheat flour

1 teaspoon salt

1 teaspoon caster sugar

1 x 7g sachet easy blend dried yeast

a little extra flour

Preheat the oven to 200°C/400°F/gas mark 6. Lightly grease and flour a 900g/2lb or 2 x 450/1lb loaf tins.

In a large bowl mix together all the ingredients. Make a well in the centre and pour in 400ml/14floz hand hot water. Combine the mixture together and work together until the bowl is clean, adding a little extra water if necessary.

Transfer the dough to a lightly floured surface, stretch to an oblong, fold both ends into the centre then shape to fit the tin. If using 2 smaller tins then first cut the dough in 2 and then shape to fit the tins.

Sprinkle the surface of the loaf/s with a little flour. Cover with a damp cloth and leave to rise for about 40 minutes or until doubled in size. Bake for 30 minutes for smaller loaves and 40 minutes for a larger loaf. Cool for about 20 minutes before slicing.

PER SERVING

energy	protein	carbohydrate	fat
144 kcal	**6** grams	**30** grams	**1** gram

Granary loaf

Preparation and cooking time 1½–2 hours
Serves 24 • Suitable for freezing

1kg/2.2lb granary flour

2 teaspoons salt

2 x 7g sachets easy blend dried yeast

3 tablespoons olive oil

Preheat the oven to 220°C/450°F/gas mark 8. Lightly grease and flour 2 x 900g/2lb loaf tins.

Mix together the flour, salt and yeast making a well in the centre. Mix the oil with 600ml/1 pint hand hot water and pour into the well in the centre and combine. Tip the mixture out onto a lightly floured surface and knead for 8–10 minutes until smooth and elastic. Place in a lightly greased bowl and cover with a damp cloth, leaving to rise until doubled in size. Knock back then divide the dough into 2, shape and place in the prepared tins. Cover again and leave to prove for until the dough has risen above the tins. Cook for 30–40 minutes until golden and hollow when tapped on the bottom. Leave to cool for 20 minutes before slicing. Delicious warm with a little butter and jam.

PER SERVING			
energy	protein	carbohydrate	fat
219 kcal	**8** grams	**41** grams	**4** grams

Irish soda bread

Unlike other bread recipes this is quick and easy to prepare as it requires no proving time.

Preparation and cooking time 40 minutes
Serves 8 • Suitable for freezing

250g/9oz wholemeal plain flour

200g/7oz plain flour

1/2 teaspoon bicarbonate of soda

1/2 teaspoon cream of tartar

25g/1oz butter

300ml/1/2 pint buttermilk or skimmed milk

Preheat the oven to 200°C/400°F gas mark 6.

Sift together the dry ingredients into a bowl, rub in the fat until the mixture resembles fine breadcrumbs. Quickly stir in the buttermilk and combine until a dough is formed. Turn the dough onto a lightly floured surface and knead until smooth. Shape the dough into rounds, place onto a lightly floured baking sheet, cut a cross in the top, sprinkle with a little flour then bake for 25–30 minutes.

PER SERVING			
energy	protein	carbohydrate	fat
128 kcal	**5** grams	**28** grams	**2** grams

Irish soda bread

Cheese and herb loaf

Preparation and cooking time 50 minutes
Serves 10 • Suitable for freezing

125g/4½ oz plain flour

125g/4½ oz plain wholemeal flour

1 teaspoon bicarbonate of soda

½ teaspoon cream of tartar

½ teaspoon dried mustard powder

50g/1¾oz low fat spread

4 tablespoons chopped fresh parsley

125g/4½ oz mature cheddar, grated

5 spring onions, finely chopped

1 egg, beaten

150ml/¼ pint milk

salt and freshly ground black pepper

Preheat the oven to 200°C/400°F/gas mark 6. Grease and line a 900g/2lb loaf tin.

Sift the flours, bicarbonate of soda, cream of tartar and mustard powder, tipping any bran in the sieve into the bowl.

Rub in the fat until the mixture resembles fine breadcrumbs. Stir in the parsley, two thirds of the cheese and the spring onions. Mix together the egg and the milk and season well. Pour the milk mixture into the bowl and combine well. Spoon the mixture into the prepared tin, sprinkle over the reserved cheese and bake for 35–40 minutes, until a skewer when inserted comes out clean. Allow to cool in the tin for 5 minutes before turning onto a wire rack. Serve in slices, warm or cold.

PER SERVING			
energy	protein	carbohydrate	fat
274 kcal	**8** grams	**35** grams	**12** grams

Walnut bread

Preparation and cooking time 1¼ hours plus proving
Serves 12 • Suitable for freezing

300g/10½ oz strong wholemeal flour
300g/10½ oz plain flour
1 teaspoon salt
1 x 7g sachet easy blend dried yeast
1 tablespoon soft brown sugar
175g/6oz walnut pieces
1 tablespoons walnut oil

Preheat the oven to 200°C/400°F/gas mark 6. Grease and line a 900g/2lb loaf tin.

Sift together the flours and the salt, stir in the yeast, sugar and walnuts. Mix the oil with 400ml/14fl oz hand hot water, pour into the flour and bring together to form a ball.

Tip the dough onto a lightly floured surface and knead for 5 minutes. Place the dough in a lightly oiled bowl and leave to prove in a warm place until doubled in size.

Re-knead the dough then shape and place in the prepared tin. Leave to prove until double in size then bake for 45–50 minutes.

Remove from the tin and return to the oven for 5 minutes. Cool on a wire rack.

PER SERVING

energy	protein	carbohydrate	fat
172 kcal	**7** grams	**18** grams	**8** grams

Bacon, leek and potato scones

Ideal served with soups or used to accompany a salad for a light lunch.

Preparation and cooking time 40 minutes
Makes 10 • Suitable for freezing

1 tablespoon oil

3 slices lean back bacon, finely chopped

1 leek, finely chopped

175g/6oz plain flour

2 teaspoons baking powder

50g/1¾oz butter

125g/4½oz mashed potato

50g/1¾oz fresh parmesan cheese, grated

2 tablespoons fresh thyme, chopped

2 tablespoons milk

1 small egg yolk, beaten

salt and freshly ground black pepper

Preheat the oven to 220°C/425°F/gas mark 7.

Heat the oil in a non-stick frying pan add the bacon and leek and fry for 3–4 minutes until the bacon is crisp. Sift the flour and baking powder into a large bowl, add the butter and rub in until the mixture resembles fine breadcrumbs. Season and add all the remaining ingredients except the egg and combine well until a soft dough is formed.

Tip out the dough onto a lightly floured surface and press or roll out to a thickness of 1½cm/¾inch. Using a 6cm fluted cutter stamp out about 10 scones. Brush with a little beaten egg then bake for 10–15 minutes until golden and risen. Cool on a wire rack and serve warm or cold.

PER SERVING			
energy	protein	carbohydrate	fat
158 kcal	**6** grams	**16** grams	**8** grams

Bacon, leek and potato scones

Malted wholemeal bloomer

Preparation and cooking time 1½ hours
Serves 12 • Suitable for freezing

350g/12oz malted wholemeal flour

125g/4½oz strong plain flour

75g/2¾oz sunflower seeds, toasted

50g/2¾oz pumpkin seeds, toasted

2 teaspoons salt

2 teaspoon light soft brown sugar

1 x 7g sachet easy blend dried yeast

150ml/¼ pint skimmed milk mixed with an equal amount of hand hot water

2 tablespoons oil

1 small egg yolk, beaten

Preheat the oven to 220°C/425°F/gas mark 7.

Sift together the flours, tipping any bran in the sieve back into the bowl. Stir in all but 2 tablespoons of the seeds, salt, sugar and yeast.

Mix together the milk mixture and the oil and stir into the flour and combine. Turn out onto a lightly floured surface and knead for 8–10 minutes until smooth and elastic. Place in a lightly oiled bowl, cover and leave to rise until doubled in size.

Knock back the dough and shape into a round. Make 4 or 5 slashes across the top with a sharp knife, cover with a damp cloth and leave to prove for 15 minutes until doubled in size, brush with a little beaten egg and sprinkle over the reserved seeds.

Bake for 10 minutes then reduce the temperature to 200°C/400°F/gas mark 6 and continue to cook for 25 minutes until golden and hollow when tapped. Cool on a wire rack.

PER SERVING			
energy	protein	carbohydrate	fat
214 kcal	**8** grams	**30** grams	**8** grams

Muesli bread

Preparation and cooking time 1½ hours
Serves 8 • Not suitable for freezing

125g/4½oz reduced sugar muesli

75g/2¾oz ready-to-eat dried apricots

150ml/¾ pint warm skimmed milk

75g/2¾oz rye flour

300g strong white flour

1 teaspoon salt

1 teaspoon easy blend dried yeast

1 teaspoon caster sugar

1 small egg, beaten

25g/1oz sunflower seeds

Preheat the oven to 200°C/400°F/gas mark 6.

Mix together the muesli, apricots and milk and leave aside for 10 minutes.

Sift together the flours, tipping any bran in the sieve back into the bowl. Stir in the salt, yeast and sugar. Make a well in the centre add the muesli mixture and 200ml/7 f l o z hand hot water, mix together to form a soft dough adding a little extra water if necessary.

Turn the dough out onto a lightly floured surface and knead for 6–7 minutes until smooth and elastic. Place in a lightly oiled bowl, cover and leave to rise until doubled in size.

Knock back the dough then shape into an oblong. Cover and leave to prove for 20 minutes. Brush the dough with a little egg then sprinkle over the seeds.

Bake for 40–45 minutes, until golden and hollow when tapped. Cool on a wire rack.

PER SERVING			
energy	protein	carbohydrate	fat
259 kcal	**9** grams	**50** grams	**3** grams

Naan

Naan is traditionally cooked on the walls of a hot clay oven or 'tandoor'. Delicious eaten with any Indian meal or as a snack.

Preparation and cooking time 25 minutes plus rising
Makes 6 • Not suitable for freezing

150ml/¾ pint hand hot milk

2 teaspoon caster sugar

2 teaspoon dried active yeast

450g/1lb plain flour

pinch salt

1 teaspoon baking powder

2 tablespoons oil

150g carton natural yogurt

1 egg, beaten

Preheat the oven to 240°C/475°F/gas mark 9. Place a heavy baking sheet in the oven.

Put the milk into a bowl, add half of the sugar and the yeast. Set aside for 20 minutes, until the mixture is frothy.

Sift together the flour, salt and baking powder, add the oil, yogurt, egg, remaining sugar and the yeast mixture. Mix to form a ball of dough. Tip out onto a lightly floured surface and knead for 8–10 minutes until smooth and elastic. Place in a lightly oiled bowl, cover with cling film and leave in a warm place for 1 hour, or until doubled in size.

Knock back the dough and divide into 6 pieces. Cover up 5 of the pieces and in turn, shape into tear shapes about 25cm/10 inch long by 12cm/5 inch wide. Slap the dough onto the preheated baking sheet and cook for 3–4 minutes until puffed up. Place under a hot grill for about 30 seconds or until golden. Keep warm and cook the other pieces of dough in the same way. Serve hot.

PER SERVING			
energy	protein	carbohydrate	fat
298 kcal	**19.1** grams	**28** grams	**12.4** grams

Mini dinner rolls

Preparation and cooking time 1½ hours
Makes 18 • Suitable for freezing

750g/1½lb strong plain flour
1 teaspoon salt
1 x 7g sachet easy blend dried yeast
1 tablespoon olive oil
450ml/¾ pint warm water
100g/3½oz black olives, chopped
a little milk for brushing
poppy seeds

Preheat the oven to 200°C/400°F/gas mark 6.

Mix together the flour, salt and yeast in a large bowl. Stir the oil into the warm water and pour over the flour. Combine to form a soft dough, tip out onto a lightly floured surface and knead for 5 minutes until smooth.

Place in a lightly oiled bowl, cover and leave to rise for about an hour until doubled in size. Tip out the risen dough and knead in the olives. Form into 18 rolls, cover, then leave to prove until doubled in size.

Brush with a little milk, sprinkle over the poppy seeds, then bake for 15–20 minutes until golden and hollow when tapped.

Cool then serve.

PER SERVING

energy	protein	carbohydrate	fat
153 kcal	**4** grams	**32** grams	**2** grams

Biscuits & other bakes

Biscuits are a traditional between meal snack as they are cheap and convenient to eat. There is a huge variety of ready-made or home made to choose from.

Most biscuits are a source saturated animal fat or hydrogenated vegetable fat – which is linked to heart disease, so filling up on too many biscuits is not advisable.

Digestives, cream-filled and shortbread are all examples of biscuits with a higher fat content, whereas garibaldi, rich tea and fig rolls have a lower fat content.

Our recipes have been adapted to be lower in fat than their standard versions.

However, all biscuits will add a significant amount of calories and fat to your diet if you eat too many. But, when you do want to indulge, nothing beats melt in the mouth home baked biscuits.

Florentines

Preparation and cooking time 30 minutes
Suitable for freezing before brushing with chocolate
Makes about 32 • Not suitable for freezing

50g/1³/₄oz butter

100g/3½oz caster sugar

75g/2³/₄oz flaked almonds

75g/2³/₄oz blanched almonds, roughly chopped

5 glace cherries

8 ready-to-eat dried apricots

100g/3½oz plain chocolate, melted

Preheat the oven to 180°C/350°F/gas mark 4. Line baking sheets with baking parchment.

Place the butter in a small pan and melt, add the sugar and heat gently, until dissolved, then boil for 1 minute. Add the remaining ingredients, except the chocolate and stir well.

Spoon small amounts of the mixture on to the baking sheets, allowing enough room for them to spread. Bake for about 10 minutes until golden. Remove from the oven and, using a knife, neaten up the edges. Leave to cool then remove from the baking sheet. Brush the backs of the florentines with a little chocolate and leave to set.

PER SERVING			
energy	protein	carbohydrate	fat
71 kcal	**1** grams	**10** grams	**3** grams

Gluten free chocolate and nut cookies

Preparation and cooking time 30 minutes plus chilling
Makes 14 • Not suitable for freezing

75g/2³/₄oz cornflour

75g/2³/₄oz rice flour

50g/1³/₄oz icing sugar

75g/2³/₄oz low fat spread

1 medium egg yolk

40g/1½oz hazelnuts, toasted and roughly chopped

25g/1oz gluten free plain chocolate, roughly chopped

1 tablespoon milk

Preheat the oven to 190°C/375°F/gas mark 5.

Place the cornflour, rice flour and icing sugar into a bowl, then, using your fingertips, rub in the low fat spread until the mixture resembles fine breadcrumbs.

Stir in the remaining ingredients and make into a ball. Wrap in clingfilm and chill for about 30 minutes. Roll out the dough to a thickness of ½cm/¼ inch and cut into 6cm/2½ inch rounds. Place the rounds onto a non-stick baking sheet and cook for 15–20 minutes or until golden. Cool on a wire rack.

PER SERVING			
energy	protein	carbohydrate	fat
298 kcal	**19.1** grams	**28** grams	**12.4** grams

Gluten free chocolate and nut cookies

White chocolate and orange cookies

Preparation and cooking time 25 minutes
Makes 16 • Keep for 2–3 days in an air tight container

125g/4½oz margarine
50g/1¾oz soft brown sugar
50g/1¾oz white chocolate drops or block chocolate, chopped
grated rind and juice 1 orange
75g/2¾oz plain wholemeal flour
75g/2¾oz plain flour

Preheat the oven to 180°C/350°F/gas mark 4. Lightly grease two baking sheets.

In a bowl beat together the margarine and sugar until light. Stir in the remaining ingredients and combine well. Divide the mixture onto the baking sheets and press down lightly with the back of a fork. Bake for 15 minutes until golden. Cool slightly on the baking sheet, then transfer to a wire rack.

PER SERVING			
energy	protein	carbohydrate	fat
119 kcal	**1** grams	**13** grams	**7** grams

Apple and oat slices

Preparation and cooking time 45 minutes
Serves 16 • Not suitable for freezing

450g/1lb cooking apples, peeled, cored and sliced

2 tablespoons caster sugar

250g/8oz reduced fat spread

2 tablespoons runny honey

175g/6oz plain wholemeal flour

1 teaspoon baking powder

200g/7oz rolled oats

50g/1¾oz chopped hazelnuts

Preheat the oven to 180°C/350°F/gas mark 4. Lightly grease a 18 x 27cm/7 x 11 inch shallow tin.

Place the apples into a pan with the sugar and 2 tablespoons water. Bring to the boil and simmer gently until softened. Remove from the heat.

Melt the reduced fat spread in a large saucepan and stir in the honey. Remove from the heat and stir in the flour, baking powder, oats and nuts.

Press half of the oat mixture into the tray. Spoon the apple mixture over the oats and smooth out. Crumble over the remaining oat mixture and press down lightly. Bake for 30 minutes or until browned. Allow to cool in the tin slightly, then cut into 16 bars and cool on a wire rack.

PER SERVING			
energy	protein	carbohydrate	fat
203 kcal	**2** grams	**23** grams	**11** grams

Chocolate brownies

Preparation and cooking time 40 minutes
Makes 16 • Suitable for freezing

225g/8 oz plain chocolate

75g/2¾oz dried dates

1 tablespoon baking powder

½ teaspoon bicarbonate of soda

75g/2¾oz soft dark brown sugar

1 medium egg, beaten

150g/5½oz self-raising flour

3 tablespoons skimmed milk

50g/1¾oz pecan nuts or walnuts

Preheat the oven to 180°C/350°F/gas Mark 4. Grease and line a 17 x 27cm/7 x 11 inch baking tin.

Melt the chocolate over a pan of simmering water. Place the dates in a pan with 6 tablespoons water, simmer gently until they form a purée. Combine all the ingredients together in a large bowl then transfer to the prepared tin. Smooth the surface. Bake in the oven for 25–30 minutes until just firm to the touch. Cut into 16 squares and serve.

PER SERVING			
energy	protein	carbohydrate	fat
102 kcal	**1** grams	**14** grams	**5** grams

Chocolate brownies

Chocolate and fruit crunchies

Preparation time 15 minutes plus chilling
Makes 12 • Keep for up to one week in foil

75g/2¾oz butter or margarine

3 tablespoons golden syrup

2 tablespoons cocoa powder

200g/7oz digestive or oat biscuits, roughly crushed

100g/3½oz ready-to-eat dried apricots, roughly chopped

50g/1¾oz sultanas

50g/1¾oz glacé cherries, chopped

In a small pan melt together the butter, syrup and cocoa powder. Stir in the biscuits, and dried fruit then press into a 20cm/8inch sandwich tin. Chill for about 1 hour until set.

Cut into 12 wedges and serve.

PER SERVING			
energy	protein	carbohydrate	fat
171 kcal	**3** grams	**25** grams	**7** grams

Mincemeat slices

Preparation and cooking time 30 minutes
Makes 12 • Suitable for freezing

100g/3½oz plain flour

100g/3½oz rolled oats

100g/3½oz soft light brown sugar

100g/3½oz margarine

411g/14oz jar mincemeat

Preheat the oven to 200°C/400°F/gas mark 6. Lightly grease a 23 x 23cm square baking tin.

In a bowl mix together the flour, oats and sugar. Add the margarine and rub in until the mixture resembles fine breadcrumbs. Press half the mixture into the tin, spread over the mincemeat, then crumble over the remaining oat mixture and press down lightly.

Bake for 20–25 minutes until golden. Remove from the oven and cut into 16 squares. Cool and serve.

PER SERVING			
energy	protein	carbohydrate	fat
106 kcal	**3** grams	**7.2** grams	**8** grams

Macaroons

Preparation and cooking time 25 minutes
Makes 30 • Not suitable for freezing

| 2 egg yolks |
| 1 egg white |
| 200g/7oz icing sugar |
| 2 teaspoons baking powder |
| grated rind 1 (half) lemon |
| a few drops vanilla essence |
| 350g/12oz ground almonds |
| a little oil for greasing |

Preheat the oven to 180°C/350°F/gas mark 4. Lightly grease baking sheets.

Beat together the egg yolks, egg white, icing sugar, baking powder, lemon rind and vanilla essence. Stir in enough ground almonds to give a stiff paste, then form into a ball. Roll about 30 walnut sized pieces of mixture into balls, flatten slightly on a lightly icing sugared surface, then place onto the prepared baking sheets about 3cm apart.

Bake for 12–15 minutes until golden. Remove from the tray and cool on a wire rack.

PER SERVING			
energy	protein	carbohydrate	fat
185 kcal	**2** grams	**32** grams	**7** grams

Cakes

Shop bought cakes and those baked for special occasions may be high in sugar, but remember that even though a whole cake may contain 8oz sugar, if that cake is cut into 14 or 16 pieces then the amount of sugar in one portion is really quite small.

With everyday cakes, try to reduce the amount of sugar used and to incorporate more high fibre ingredients like, wholemeal flour, oatmeal, fruit (fresh or dried), nuts, vegetables (like carrots) and seeds (poppy, sesame, etc).

A few of the most important tips when baking a cake are:

- Always use the correct size and depth of tin. If you are using a square tin instead of a round one then use one that is 2½ cm or 1 inch smaller, eg for an 8 inch round cake tin use a 7 inch square one.

- Never mix imperial and metric measures. Stick to one or the other.

- Ensure you have an accurate set of weighing scales and measure ingredients carefully.

- Always preheat your oven to the required temperature. Remember cooking times will vary depending on your oven.

- Don't open the door once the cake is in the oven or it will sink!

> For everyday cakes try to incorporate more **high fibre** ingredients... "

Basic cake methods

There are a number of methods to make cakes, but to ensure good flavour, texture and appearance it is necessary to take some time with the initial preparation.

Rub in

The fat is rubbed into the flour. This method is economical and allows you to cut down on the fat and sugar in the recipe. You use this method when making, for example, scones.

Cream

Sugar is necessary for bulk. Fat and sugar are creamed together until light and fluffy, incorporating air in the process. An example of when this method is used is when making a Victoria sandwich sponge.

Whisk

Eggs and sugar are whisked until thick, incorporating a lot of air, for example when making Swiss rolls. This allows fat to be left out completely.

Lemon crumble cake

Preparation and cooking time 1¼ hours
Serves 16 • Suitable for freezing
For the crumble

50g/1¾oz golden granulated sugar

25g/1oz plain flour

grated rind 1 lemon

25g/1oz butter

For the cake

225g/8 oz plain flour

½ teaspoon bicarbonate of soda

grated rind and juice 1 lemon

100g/3½ oz butter

125g/5½ oz caster sugar

225g/8 oz buttermilk

2 eggs lightly beaten

Preheat the oven to 180°C/350°/gas mark 4. Lightly grease and line a 900g/2lb loaf tin.

To make the crumble mixture, in a bowl stir together the sugar, flour and lemon rind, rub in the butter, until the mixture resembles coarse breadcrumbs. Set aside.

For the cake, sift together the flour and bicarbonate of soda into a bowl. Stir in the lemon rind. Place the butter and lemon juice into a pan and heat until melted. Stir in the sugar, buttermilk and eggs. Pour into the flour mixture and combine well. Pour into the tin, smooth out then sprinkle over the crumble mixture and press down lightly.

Bake for about 1 hour or until well risen and golden. Leave to cool in the tin for about 30 minutes, then serve.

PER SERVING			
energy	protein	carbohydrate	fat
186 kcal	**3** grams	**26** grams	**8** grams

Coffee and walnut sponge

Preparation and cooking time 1 hour 10 minutes
Serves 10 • Not suitable for freezing

For the cake

175g/6oz walnut pieces, roughly chopped and toasted

75g/2¾oz plain flour

5 eggs, separated

175g/6oz caster sugar

For the filling

150ml/¼ pint whipping cream

2 tablespoons fromage frais

2 teaspoons coffee dissolved in 1 teaspoon boiling water

2 tablespoon icing sugar

To decorate

a little icing sugar

Preheat the oven to 180°C/350°F/gas mark 4. Grease and line an 20cm/8inch spring-form tin.

Place the walnuts and flour into a food processor or blender and blend to a fine powder.

In a large bowl whisk together the egg yolks and sugar until they are pale and thick and a trail is left when the whisk is lifted. Gently fold through the flour mixture.

Whisk the egg whites until they form soft peaks, then fold through the egg yolk mixture. Pour into the prepared tin, then bake for 45–50 minutes until just firm to the touch. Cool, then remove from the tin and slice the cake into two.

Whip the cream until it forms soft peaks, stir through the fromage frais, coffee mixture and the icing sugar and spoon onto one of the cake halves then sandwich together. Dust with a little icing sugar and serve.

PER SERVING			
energy	protein	carbohydrate	fat
263 kcal	**6** grams	**21** grams	**15** grams

Coconut and cherry loaf

Preparation and cooking time 1 hour
Serves 14 • Suitable for freezing

125g/4½ oz unsalted butter

75g/2¾ oz caster sugar

3 eggs, separated

1 teaspoon vanilla extract

125g/4½ oz self-raising flour

50g/1¾ oz desiccated coconut

125g/4½ oz glacé cherries, chopped

2 tablespoons demerara sugar

Preheat the oven to 180°C/350°F/gas mark 4. Grease and base line a 900g/2lb loaf tin.

Beat together the butter and caster sugar until light and fluffy. Gradually beat in the egg yolks and the vanilla essence. Fold in the flour, coconut and glacé cherries. Whisk the egg whites until they form soft peaks, then fold gently into the other mixture.

Spoon into the prepared tin. Sprinkle over the demerara sugar then bake for about 45 minutes until golden. Cool in the tin then serve.

PER SERVING

energy	protein	carbohydrate	fat
187 kcal	**5** grams	**30** grams	**5** grams

Banana, oat and walnut muffins

Preparation and cooking time 30 minutes
Serves 12 • Suitable for freezing

250g/9oz plain flour

75g/2¾ oz rolled oats

1 tablespoon baking powder

¼ teaspoon grated nutmeg

2 medium bananas, mashed

75g/2¾ oz walnut pieces

1 egg, beaten

75g/2¾ oz butter, melted

25g/1 oz light muscavado sugar

175ml/6floz buttermilk

3 tablespoons runny honey

Preheat the oven to 200°C/400°F/gas mark 6. Lightly grease and flour 12 muffin tins.

In a large bowl mix together the flour, oats, baking powder and nutmeg. Mix together all the remaining ingredients and fold through the flour until just combined. Spoon into the prepared tins and bake for about 20 minutes until risen and golden. Cool in the tin for 10 minutes the serve.

PER SERVING			
energy	protein	carbohydrate	fat
187 kcal	**19.1** grams	**28** grams	**12.4** grams

Moist carrot cake

Preparation and cooking time 45 minutes
Cuts into 16 pieces • Suitable for freezing before adding topping
For the cake

125g/4¹/₂ oz dark soft brown sugar

2 eggs

100ml/3¹/₂ fl oz sunflower oil

175g/6oz wholemeal self-raising flour

1¹/₂ teaspoons bicarbonate of soda

1 teaspoon ground cinnamon

grated rind and juice 1 orange

1 large carrots, peeled and grated

150g/4¹/₂ oz ready-to-eat dried apricots, chopped
For the topping

1 x 200g pack extra light cream cheese

1 tablespoon icing sugar

few drops vanilla essence

a little ground cinnamon

Preheat the oven to 180°C/350°F/gas mark 4. Lightly grease and line a 23 x 23cm/9 x 9 inches baking tin.

In a large bowl whisk together the sugar, eggs and oil for 1–2 minutes. Sift the flour, bicarbonate of soda and the cinnamon into the bowl, tipping in any bran that remains in the sieve. Stir through the remaining cake ingredients. Pour the mixture into the prepared tin.

Cook for 25–30 minutes, until just firm to the touch. Cool on a wire rack. Meanwhile, beat together all the topping ingredients, except the cinnamon. When the cake is cool, smooth the topping over the cake, sprinkle over a little cinnamon and serve.

| PER SERVING | | | |
energy	protein	carbohydrate	fat
298 kcal	**19.1** grams	**28** grams	**12.4** grams

Banana and pecan loaf

Preparation and cooking time 1¼ hours
Serves 4 • Suitable for freezing

75g/2¾ oz plain flour

75g/2¾ oz wholemeal flour

1 teaspoon bicarbonate of soda

1 teaspoon ground mixed spice

100g/3½ oz butter, softened

100g/3½ oz caster sugar

2 large bananas, mashed

2 eggs lightly beaten

100g/3½ oz pecan nuts, roughly chopped

Preheat the oven to 180°C/350°F/gas mark 4. Grease and line a 900g/2lb loaf tin.

Sift together the flours, bicarbonate of soda and mixed spice, tipping any bran in the sieve into the bowl.

In a large bowl beat together the butter and sugar until light and fluffy. Beat in the bananas and egg then stir in the flour mixture along with 5 tablespoons boiling water. Stir in the pecan nuts.

Spoon the mixture into the tin and smooth out the top. Bake for about 1 hour until risen and golden. Cool on a wire rack. Delicious served warm.

| PER SERVING | | | |
energy	protein	carbohydrate	fat
225 kcal	**4** grams	**23** grams	**12** grams

Banana & pecan loaf

American bran muffins

Preparation and cooking time 25 minutes
Makes 12 • **Suitable for freezing**

250g/9 oz oatbran
50g/1¾ oz sultanas
1 tablespoon caster sugar
1 teaspoon ground cinnamon
1 tablespoon baking powder
2 tablespoons oil
2 medium egg whites
350ml/12 fl oz skimmed milk

Preheat the oven to 220°C/425°F/gas mark 7.

Mix together the oatbran, sultanas, sugar, cinnamon and baking powder. In a separate bowl mix the remaining ingredients, pour over the bran mixture and mix well. Set the mixture aside for 5 minutes then divide between 12 muffin cases set in a muffin tray. Bake in the oven for 12–15 minutes until golden and risen.

PER SERVING

energy	protein	carbohydrate	fat
123 kcal	**4** grams	**20** grams	**3** grams

Blackberry and pear cake

Preparation and cooking time 1¼ hours
Serves 10 • **Suitable for freezing**

150g/5½ oz self-raising flour
2 teaspoon baking powder
75g/2¾ oz margarine
50g/1¾ oz ground almonds
2 eggs
grated rind and juice 1 orange
few drops almond essence
2 pears, peeled, cored and chopped
125g/4½ oz blackberries
1 tablespoon demerara sugar

Preheat the oven to 200°C/400°F/gas mark 6. Line a deep 20cm / 8 inch cake tin.

In a large bowl beat together the flour, baking powder, margarine, almonds, eggs, orange rind and juice and the almond essence.

Fold through the pears and blackberries, then spoon the mixture into the prepared tin. Sprinkle over the demerara sugar then bake for 45 minutes–1 hour until firm to touch. Cool and serve.

PER SERVING

energy	protein	carbohydrate	fat
187 kcal	**4** grams	**17** grams	**11** grams

Madeira cake

Preparation and cooking time 1¼ hours
Serves 12 • Suitable for freezing

125g/4½oz plain flour

125g/4½oz self-raising flour

175g/6oz low fat spread

125g/4½oz caster sugar

1 teaspoon vanilla extract

3 eggs, beaten

grated rind and juice 1 lemon

Preheat the oven to 180°C/350°F/gas mark 4. Grease and line a deep 18cm/7inch cake tin.

Sift together the flours into a large bowl. Cream together the low fat spread and the sugar until light and fluffy. Beat in the vanilla essence. Add the eggs a little at a time, beating well after each addition. Fold in the flour using a spoon then stir through the lemon rind and juice.

Spoon the mixture into the prepared tin and level the surface. Bake for about 1 hour or until golden and firm to the touch. Cool on a wire rack then serve.

PER SERVING

energy	protein	carbohydrate	fat
186 kcal	**5** grams	**25** grams	**7** grams

Ginger fruit tea bread

Preparation and cooking time 1 hour plus soaking overnight
Serves 14 • Suitable for freezing

175ml/6floz strong black tea
175g/6oz sultanas
175g/6oz raisins
175g/6oz ready-to-eat dried apricots, chopped
3 pieces stem ginger, chopped
3 tablespoons of the syrup
125g/4½oz soft brown sugar
1 egg, lightly beaten
25g/1oz butter melted
250g/9oz plain flour
½teaspoon bicarbonate of soda

Place the tea, fruit, stem ginger and syrup into a large bowl, stir well, cover and set aside overnight.

Preheat the oven to 180°C/350°F/gas mark 4. Grease and line a 900g/2lb loaf tin.

Stir in the remaining ingredients into the fruit and combine well. Spoon the mixture into the prepared tin. Cook for 45–50 minutes. Cool for 10 minutes in the tin then continue to cool on a wire rack.

PER SERVING			
energy	protein	carbohydrate	fat
200 kcal	**3** grams	**44** grams	**2** grams

Polenta and almond cake

Preparation and cooking time 1 hour
Serves 14 • Not suitable for freezing but will store in an airtight container for 5–6 days.

175g/6oz butter, softened
175g/6oz caster sugar
4 eggs
few drops almond essence
125g/4½oz instant polenta
100g/3½oz ground almonds

1½ teaspoons baking powder

icing sugar to dust

Preheat the oven to 180°C/350°F/gas mark 4. Lightly grease and base line a 20cm/8 inch deep cake tin.

Place all the ingredients except the icing sugar into a large bowl and, using a hand whisk, beat until light and fluffy.

Spoon into the prepared tin and level out the surface. Cook for 40–45 minutes until a skewer when inserted comes out clean. Cool in the tin for 30 minutes, then turn out onto a wire rack and dredge with icing sugar.

PER SERVING

energy	protein	carbohydrate	fat
240 kcal	**4** grams	**20** grams	**14** grams

Chocolate sponge

Make the basic Victoria sponge (see page 56) replacing 25g/1oz flour with 25g/1oz cocoa powder. Fill with a little whipped cream and dust with a mixture of icing sugar and cocoa powder.

Lemon and lime sponge

Make the basic Victoria sponge (see page 56) and add the grated rind and juice of 1 lime. Whip together 150ml/¼ pint whipping cream, the grated rind and juice of 1 lemon and 1 tablespoon icing sugar. Use the mixture to sandwich together the 2 sponge halves then dust with a little icing sugar.

Mango and passion fruit sponge

Make the basic Victoria sponge (see page 56). Whip 150ml/¼ pint whipping cream until it forms stiff peaks and fold through 2 tablespoons fromage frais and the flesh of 2 passion fruit. Smooth over one of the sponge halves then top with the chopped flesh of 1 mango. Top with the remaining sponge and dust with a little icing sugar.

Basic all-in-one Victoria sandwich cake

Preparation and cooking time 45 minutes
Serves 10 • **Suitable for freezing before decorating**
For the cake

150g/6oz self-raising flour

1 teaspoon baking powder

3 eggs

150g/6oz butter or margarine

100g/3½ oz caster sugar

few drops vanilla essence

To decorate

a little jam

icing sugar

Preheat the oven to 180°C/350°F/gas mark 4. Grease and line two 20cm/8 inch sponge tins.

Sift together the flour and baking powder. Add all the remaining ingredients to the bowl and using an electric hand whisk beat until you have a smooth mixture. The mixture should be fairly stiff but it should fall off the spoon when tapped. If the mixture seems a little too stiff add a little water and whisk again. Divide the mixture between the 2 sponge tins and smooth the top. Cook for 30–35 minutes until golden and risen and the surface springs back when touched. Remove from the tin and cool on a wire rack. Sandwich together with a little jam and dust with icing sugar.

PER SERVING			
energy	protein	carbohydrate	fat
226 kcal	**4** grams	**22** grams	**12** grams

Fresh fruit and yogurt cake

A really simple cake, use the yogurt carton to measure out the other cake ingredients
Preparation and cooking time 40 minutes
Serves 12 • **Cakes suitable for freezing before decorating**

Basic all-in-one Victoria sandwich cake

For the cake

150g/5½ oz carton strawberry yogurt

1 carton caster sugar

1 carton sunflower oil

1 carton plain flour

2 tablespoons baking powder

4 eggs

2 tablespoons strawberry jam

To decorate

142ml carton whipping cream

4 tablespoons Greek yogurt

250g/8oz fresh fruit eg strawberries, raspberries and blueberries

a little icing sugar for dusting

Preheat the oven to 200°C/400°F/gas mark 6. Grease and lightly flour two 20cm/8 inch sandwich tins.

In a large bowl or food processor blend together all the cake ingredients until smooth, divide between the 2 prepared tins. Bake for 25–30 minutes, until golden and firm to the touch. Remove from the tins and leave to cool.

Whip the cream until it forms soft peaks and stir though the Greek yogurt. Spoon the cream mixture over one of the sponges, layer over the fruit and sandwich together with the other sponge. Dust with a little icing sugar and serve.

PER SERVING			
energy	protein	carbohydrate	fat
290 kcal	**6** grams	**33** grams	**13** grams

Gingerbread

Preparation and cooking time 1¼ hours
Serves 20 • Suitable for freezing

125g/4½oz butter

100g/3½oz dark muscavado sugar

150g/5½oz golden syrup

225g/8oz plain flour

4 teaspoon ground ginger

1 teaspoon bicarbonate of soda

150ml/½ pint milk

1 egg, beaten

4 pieces preserved ginger, finely chopped

Preheat the oven to 160°C/325°F/Gas mark 3. Lightly grease and base line an 18cm/7inch square cake tin.

Place the butter, sugar, syrup, flour, ginger, bicarbonate of soda, milk and egg into a large bowl. Using an electric hand whisk, whisk for 2–3 minutes until thoroughly combined. Stir in the preserved ginger, then pour the mixture into the cake tin and bake for about 1 hour until firm and a skewer when inserted comes out clean. Cool for a few minutes in the tin then remove and cool on a wire rack. Cut into 20 squares.

PER SERVING

energy	protein	carbohydrate	fat
132kcal	**2** grams	**20** grams	**5** grams

Panettone

Preparation and cooking time: 2½ hours
Serves 14 • Suitable for freezing, best eaten the same day

450g/1lb strong plain flour

pinch of salt

1 x 7g sachet easy blend dried yeast

75g/2oz caster sugar

25g/1oz mixed peel

100g/3½ oz sultanas

grated rind 1 orange

100g/3½ oz butter or margarine, melted

150ml/¼ pint hand hot milk

2 eggs, beaten

Preheat the oven to 180°C/350°F/gas mark 4.

Sift together the flour and salt, stir in the yeast, sugar, peel, sultanas and orange rind. Make a well in the centre and pour in the butter and milk and stir together. Add enough egg to make a soft but not sticky dough, reserving a little for brushing. Cover with oiled plastic wrap and leave in a warm place to rise for about 1 hour. Knead for 2–3 minutes using a food mixer.

Shape into a ball and place in a lightly greased 1 litre/2 pint brioche tin. Cut a cross in the top of the dough with a sharp knife. Cover and leave in a warm place to prove for 1 hour or until doubled in size. Brush the top with beaten egg. Cook for 40 minutes, cover with foil then cook for a further 20–30 minutes. Turn out and cool on a wire rack.

PER SERVING			
energy	protein	carbohydrate	fat
224 kcal	**5** grams	**36** grams	**7** grams

Chocolate roulade with raspberries

Preparation and cooking time 30 minutes
Serves 8 • Suitable for freezing
For the roulade

225g/8oz plain chocolate

5 medium eggs, separated

125g/4½oz caster sugar

For the filling

1 x 200ml carton light crème fraîche

1 tablespoon cocoa powder

250g/9oz fresh raspberries

a little icing sugar for dusting

Preheat the oven to 200°C/400°F/gas mark 6. Grease and line a 33cm x 23cm/13 x 9 inch Swiss roll tin.

Melt the chocolate in a bowl over a pan of simmering water. Whisk together the egg yolks and sugar until pale. Whisk the egg whites until stiff. Fold the chocolate and the egg whites through the egg yolk mixture. Pour into the prepared tin and cook for 15–20 minutes. Remove from the oven and cool on a wire rack. Stir together the crème fraîche, cocoa powder and the raspberries, roll up, dust with icing sugar and serve.

Variation: Use 1 orange, segmented and chopped instead of the raspberries.

PER SERVING			
energy	protein	carbohydrate	fat
400 kcal	**7.2** grams	**36.8** grams	**26** grams

Chocolate roulade with raspberries

Special

occasions

Birthdays, Christmas, Easter, christenings and weddings all mark the occasion by the sharing of a celebration cake. In general you can halve the amount of sugar in recipes and still produce delicious home baked cakes.

For special occasions, you may want to use an old favourite. Although these cakes are generally rich mixes of fat and sugar with fillings, icing and other decorations, they can still be enjoyed – in small amounts.

Tips

- Remember that rich mixes which are high in fat, keep for a reasonable amount of time so you don't have to eat them up so quickly. Have small portions only.

- Cut down on fat by using reduced or lower fat alternatives or replacements but don't compromise on flavour and texture. Using lower fat filling such as those on page 11 will be just as tasty as full cream. However a low fat spread may not work as well in creaming a mixture for a celebration cake.

- If you do eat rich celebration cakes which are normally iced, replace the icing with alternative toppings refer to pages 11 and 70.

- Don't get into the habit of having rich cakes as everyday snacks.

Celebration chocolate mousse cake

Preparation and cooking time 1½ hours
Serves 12 • Not suitable for freezing

For the cake

225g/8 oz plain chocolate, melted

1 tablespoon orange flavoured liqueur

5 eggs, separated

125g/4½ oz caster sugar

125g/4½ oz unsalted butter, softened

For the mousse

225g/8 oz plain chocolate, melted

2 tablespoons orange flavour liqueur

4 eggs, separated

icing sugar and cocoa powder to dust

Preheat the oven to 180°C/350°F/gas mark 4. Line a 20cm/8 inch spring release tin.

Make the cake by mixing together the chocolate and the liqueur. Whisk together the egg yolks and the sugar until the mixture is light and thick. Beat in the butter a little at a time, until smooth, then beat in the chocolate. Whisk the egg whites until they form stiff peaks, fold through the chocolate mixture then pour into the tin. Bake for about 40 minutes, until risen and firm. Cool for about 30 minutes in the tin, then remove and slice in half. Return the bottom half to the tin.

Make the mousse by mixing together the chocolate and the liqueur, and beat in the egg yolks. Whisk the egg whites until stiff then fold through the chocolate mixture. Pour the mousse mixture into the tin over the sponge half. Cover with clingfilm and place in the fridge until almost firm. Wrap the other sponge half in foil until required. When the mousse is almost set place on the other sponge half. Chill until firm then remove from the tin. Dust with a mixture of icing sugar and cocoa powder.

PER SERVING			
energy	protein	carbohydrate	fat
370 kcal	**7** grams	**35** grams	**22** grams

Midsummer baked cheesecake with strawberry topping

A rich dessert recipe which has been adapted to reduce fat and sugar but retaining a classic quality.

Preparation and cooking time 1 hour plus cooling
Serves 10 • Suitable for freezing before adding the raspberries
For the base

175g/6 oz oat biscuits, crushed

50g/1¾ oz butter or margarine, melted

50g/1¾ oz hazelnuts, roughly chopped

For the filling

350g/12 oz Quark

2 x 200g cartons fromage frais

3 eggs

150g/5½ oz caster sugar

1 teaspoon vanilla extract

For the topping

350g/12 oz strawberries

Preheat the oven to 150°C/300°F/gas mark 2.

Mix together all the base ingredients, until well combined, then press into the base of a 23cm/9 inch springform cake tin. Chill for 20 minutes. In a large bowl beat together all the filling ingredients, pour over the biscuit base cook for 30 minutes, then turn off the oven and leave to cool in the oven, until completely set.

Decorate with the strawberries. Also delicious if you want to use another fruit for the topping, eg apricots, raspberries or mango.

PER SERVING			
energy	protein	carbohydrate	fat
285 kcal	**12** grams	**34** grams	**12** grams

Midsummer baked cheesecake with raspberry topping

Stollen

Preparation and cooking time 2½ hours
Serves 12 • Suitable for freezing

350g/12 oz strong plain flour

1 x 7g sachet easy blend dried yeast

1 teaspoon salt

1 teaspoon mixed spice

50g/1¾oz butter

grated rind 1 orange

25g/1 oz caster sugar

100g/3½oz sultanas

50g/1¾oz ready-to-eat dried apricots

25g/1oz mixed peel

50g/1¾oz flaked almonds

1 egg, beaten

175ml/6floz warm milk

a little melted butter for brushing

150g/5½oz marzipan or almond paste (see page 70)

icing sugar to dust

Preheat the oven to 190°C/375°F/gas mark 5.

Stir together the flour, yeast, salt and spice. Rub in the butter until the mixture resembles fine breadcrumbs. Stir through the orange rind, sugar, sultanas, apricots, mixed peel and almonds. Mix together the egg and milk, pour into the flour mixture and combine to form a soft dough. Turn out onto a lightly floured surface and knead for 5–6 minutes, until smooth. Place in a lightly oiled bowl, cover with a damp cloth and leave to prove for about 1 hour until doubled in size. Knead for 1–2 minutes, then roll out to a 25cm/10 inch square. Brush with a little melted butter. Roll out the marzipan or almond paste to approximately 23 x 10cm/9 x 4 inch. Place it down the centre of the dough, fold the dough over it, cover and seal well. Place the dough seam side down on a lightly floured baking sheet, make a few slashes across the top, cover and set aside for about 30 minutes. Bake for about 35-40 minutes until hollow when tapped. Cool on a wire rack then dust with a little icing sugar before serving.

PER SERVING			
energy	protein	carbohydrate	fat
268 kcal	**7** grams	**40** grams	**10** grams

Delicious fruity Christmas cake

All rich fruit cakes are high in carbohydrate, whether they contain added sugar or not.

Preparation and cooking time
Serves 20 • Keeps for up to 3 months

175g/6oz butter, chopped

200g/7oz dark muscavado sugar

150ml/¼ pint brandy (or orange juice)

900g/1kg mixed dried fruit, eg sultanas, raisins, currants

grated rind and juice 2 oranges

100g/3½oz flaked almonds, toasted

4 eggs, beaten

150g/5½oz plain flour

150g/5½oz wholemeal flour

½ teaspoon baking powder

2 teaspoons mixed spice

Preheat the oven to 150°C/300°F/gas mark 2. Lightly grease and line a 18cm/7 inch square cake tin and tie a double thickness of greaseproof or new paper around the outside of the tin.

Place the butter, sugar, brandy, dried fruit, and orange rid and juice into a pan, place over a low heat, bring slowly to the boil, stirring. Simmer for 10 minutes, stirring occasionally.

Remove the pan from the heat and cool for about 20 minutes, then stir through the remaining ingredients until well combined. Spoon the mixture into the prepared tin, smooth out the top. Bake for 1 hour, then reduce the heat to 140°C/280°F/gas mark 1 for a further 2–2½ hours, until golden and firm. Cool then wrap in foil and store in an airtight container.

Option: make holes in the base of the cake with a skewer and drizzle over 2 tablespoon brandy and allow to soak in. Continue weekly until icing.

PER SERVING			
energy	**protein**	**carbohydrate**	**fat**
326 kcal	**6** grams	**54** grams	**11** grams

Luxury mince pies

Preparation and cooking time 2½ hours
Makes 14 • Suitable for freezing before baking

For the pastry

225g/8 oz plain flour

100g/3½ oz butter, cut into small pieces

grated rind lemon

50g/1¾ oz caster sugar

1 egg yolk

For the filling

100g/3½ oz cream cheese

grated rind and juice 1 lemon

200g/7oz luxury mincemeat

Preheat the oven to 200°C/400°F/Gas mark 6.

Put the flour, butter, lemon rind and sugar in a food processor and whizz together for about 30 seconds until the mixture resembles fine breadcrumbs. Add the egg yolk and 1 tablespoon cold water and pulse until the mixture forms a soft dough. Chill for 30 minutes.

Mix together the cream cheese and lemon rind. Stir the lemon juice through the mincemeat.

Roll out the pastry and stamp out 14 x 7½ cm/3 inch rounds , and use to line the bun tins. Spoon a teaspoon of mincemeat mixture into each pastry case, top with a spoonful of the cream cheese mixture. Roll out the remaining pastry and cut out 14 x 6 cm/2½ inch rounds , dampen the edges of the pastry and press on the lids and seal.

Bake for about 15 minutes until golden. Cool for 5 minutes in the tin then cool on a wire rack. Delicious eaten warm.

PER SERVING			
energy	protein	carbohydrate	fat
180 kcal	**2** grams	**25** grams	**8** grams

Luxury mince pies

Cake decorating

Cake decorating

There is no reason why you cannot decorate your cakes in the traditional way with almond paste and icing. The amounts in the following recipes are enough to cover an 18cm/7 inch square or a 20cm/8 inch round fruit cake

Almond paste

In a large bowl sift together 175g/6oz icing sugar and 175g/6oz caster sugar, stir in 2 eggs and 1 egg yolk, whisk until light and fluffy. Stir in a few drops almond essence, 350g/12oz ground almonds and 1 teaspoon lemon juice. Bring the mixture together to from a stiff paste. Roll out and use to cover the cake.

Royal icing

Place 3 egg whites into a large bowl and gradually stir in 500g/1lb 2oz sifted icing sugar. Then using a hand whisk, whisk for about 10 minutes until the mixture is stiff and peaky. Smooth over the cake, then using a palette knife make peaks in the icing for a snowy effect.

Butter icing

Instead of the usual butter icing which is packed with calories and saturated fat, beat a 200g/7oz carton light cream cheese with a little icing sugar and spread between the sponges.

Fruit and nut

If you prefer something a little lighter then why not brush the cake with a little apricot jam, decorate with dried fruit and nuts, then brush over with a little more apricot jam.

Other cakes

Cut down on calories! Instead of piling whipped double cream in the middle of a sponge cake, use whipping cream mixed with a little fromage frais instead. Or leave out the cream completely and fill with a luxury jam of your choice, then dust with a little icing sugar.

Cooking for children

Baking is fun for children and so is an ideal way to introduce them to food and cooking. A battle for many parents is getting kids to eat food that is nutritious for them alongside the crisps, chocolates and sweets that they want to eat.

The key is to keep children interested in food and by involving them in cooking, they can learn about different types of food. Whether it's measuring out ingredients, beating them together, kneading and shaping the bread or decorating biscuits, children can take part and will enjoy sampling the results of their hard work.

Safety and hygiene tips for children

- make sure there's always an adult in the kitchen to help you

- be careful of sharp implements like knives, and attachments for things like blenders and food processors

- oven tops and door are HOT! Always use oven gloves

- if melting things like chocolate over water be very careful of steam

- wash your hands before you start.

Easter biscuits

Preparation and cooking time 30 minutes
Makes 24 biscuits • Suitable for freezing

100g/3½ oz butter or margarine

50g/1¾ oz caster sugar

1 egg, separated

100g/3½ oz plain flour

75g/2¾ oz ground rice

1 teaspoon mixed spice

50g/1¾ oz currants

a little sugar for sprinkling

Preheat the oven to 200°C/400°F/Gas mark 6.

In a large bowl beat together the butter and sugar, until pale and creamy. Beat in the egg yolk. Fold in the remaining ingredients, except the egg white and mix to form a soft dough. Roll out on a lightly floured surface and cut into 24 rounds using a 6cm/2½ inch cutter.

Place the biscuits onto lightly floured baking sheets and bake for 10 minutes. Remove from the oven and brush with a little egg white, sprinkle over a little sugar, return to the oven and cook for a further 2–3 minutes until golden. Cool on a wire rack. **Wear your oven gloves when you are doing this.**

PER SERVING

energy	protein	carbohydrate	fat
73 kcal	**1** grams	**9** grams	**3** grams

Crunchy oat cookies

Preparation and cooking time 30 minutes
Makes 16 • Not suitable for freezing

75g/2¾ oz porridge oats

50g/1¾ oz plain flour

50g/1¾ oz margarine

50g/1¾ oz soft brown sugar

1 tablespoon golden syrup

½ teaspoon bicarbonate of soda

Preheat the oven to 180°C/350°F/gas mark 4.

In a large bowl mix together the oats and the flour. Place the margarine, sugar and syrup into a pan and heat gently until the margarine has melted and the sugar has dissolved, stir in the bicarbonate of soda. **Be very careful with the pan.**

Pour the margarine mixture into the oat mixture and stir well to combine.

Make 16 walnut sized pieces of the mixture then put them onto lightly greased baking sheets. Bake for 12–15 minutes until golden. Remove from the oven. **Wear your oven gloves when you are doing this.** Cool the cookies on the tray for a few minutes then continue to cool on a wire rack.

PER SERVING

energy	protein	carbohydrate	fat
70 kcal	**1** grams	**10** grams	**3** grams

Chocolate cracklies

Preparation and cooking time 10 minutes plus chilling
Makes 20 • Not suitable for freezing

1 king size Mars bar

25g/1oz butter or margarine

75g/2¾oz rice krispies or cornflakes

Place the Mars bar and the butter in a small pan, place over a low heat and stir until melted. **Make sure an adult helps you with this.**

Stir in the rice crispies or cornflakes, then spoon the mixture into 20 paper cases and chill until firm.

PER SERVING

energy	protein	carbohydrate	fat
45 kcal	**0** grams	**7** grams	**2** grams

Chocolate cracklies

Chocolate and raisin cookies

Preparation and cooking time 30 minutes
Makes 24 • Not suitable for freezing

150g/5½oz margarine
75g/2¾oz soft light brown sugar
1 medium egg, beaten
1 teaspoon vanilla essence
75g/2¾oz plain wholemeal flour
1 teaspoon mixed spice
½ teaspoon bicarbonate of soda
150g/5½oz rolled oats
50g/1¾oz raisins
50g/1¾oz chocolate chips or chocolate cut into small pieces

Preheat the oven to 180°/350°F/gas mark 5. Line baking sheets with greaseproof paper or baking parchment.

Cream together the margarine and sugar. Beat in the egg, 2 tablespoons water and the vanilla essence. Sift together the flour, spice and bicarbonate of soda, tipping any bran in the sieve into the bowl. Stir through the oats, raisins and chocolate, then stir into the egg mixture.

Place walnut-sized pieces of the cookie mixture onto the prepared baking sheets and flatten slightly with the back of a fork. Bake for 10–15 minutes until golden. Remove from the oven and cool on a wire rack. **Wear your oven gloves when you are doing this.**

PER SERVING			
energy	protein	carbohydrate	fat
113 kcal	**2** grams	**13** grams	**6** grams

Fruit buttermilk scones

Preparation and cooking time ½ hour
Makes 18 • Suitable for freezing

75g/2¾ oz butter

350g/12oz self-raising flour

1 teaspoon ground mixed spice

50g/1¾ oz caster sugar

75g/2¾ oz ready-to-eat dried apricots

50g/1¾ oz sultanas

175ml/6floz buttermilk

2 tablespoons milk

Preheat the oven to 200°C/400°F/gas mark 6.

Sift the flour and spice into a bowl, rub in the butter until the mixture resembles fine breadcrumbs. Stir in the sugar, apricots and sultanas.

Pour in the buttermilk and quickly stir in with a knife. The mixture may look a little dry, but don't add any extra liquid. Lightly work the mixture into a ball.

Roll out to a thickness of 2cm. Cut out approximately 18 x 4cm rounds using a plain cutter. Place the scones on a floured baking tray, brush the tops of the scones with the milk, then bake for 12–15 minutes until lightly golden. **Wear your oven gloves when you are doing this.**

Cool then serve with raspberry jam and a little light crème fraîche or extra thick single cream.

PER SERVING			
energy	protein	carbohydrate	fat
124 kcal	**2.4** grams	**21.6** grams	**3.8** grams

Basic mini muffins

Preparation and cooking time 30 minutes
Makes 36 • Not suitable for freezing

250/9 oz plain flour
2 teaspoons baking powder
½ teaspoon bicarbonate of soda
1 teaspoon vanilla essence
2 eggs beaten
284 ml/10 floz carton butter milk
50g/1¾ light soft brown sugar
75g/2¾oz butter melted

Preheat the oven to 200°C/400°F/gas mark 6.

In a large bowl sift together the flour, baking powder and bicarbonate of soda.

Whisk together the remaining ingredients and quickly fold into the flour mixture.

Spoon into lightly greased and floured mini muffin tins and bake for 15–20 minutes until risen and golden. Cool in the tin for 10 minutes then remove from the tin and cool on a wire rack.

PER SERVING			
energy	protein	carbohydrate	fat
69 kcal	**2** grams	**8** grams	**3** grams

Basic muffins

index

Further information

The Diabetes UK Careline offers help and support on all aspects of diabetes. We provide a confidential service which takes general enquiries from people with diabetes, their carers and from healthcare professionals. Our trained staff can give you the latest information on topics such as care of your diabetes, blood glucose levels, diet, illness, pregnancy, insurance, driving, welfare benefits and employment.

If you would like further information on any aspect of diabetes telephone or write to Diabetes UK Careline:

10 Queen Anne Street, London W1G 9LH

Telephone 020 7636 6112
(operates Language Line, for non-English speaking callers)

Minicom 020 7462 2757

Fax 020 7462 2732

Email careline@diabetes.org.uk

Further Diabetes UK cookbooks
- Everyday cookery – healthy recipes for the older person (2021) £4.95

- Creative recipes for all occasions (2025) £4.95

- Managing your weight – a balanced approach (2026) £4.95

- Festive foods and easy entertaining (2027) £4.95

The Diabetes UK *Catalogue* descibes our full range of books and leaflets. For copies of this and other Diabetes UK leaflets, please contact:

Diabetes UK, Distribution Department, PO Box 1, Portishead, Bristol BS20 7EG

Telephone freephone 0800 585088

Diabetes UK national and regional offices

Diabetes UK is active at a national and regional level.

Diabetes UK, Central Office
London: 020 7323 1531

Diabetes UK North West
Warrington: 01925 653281

Diabetes UK West Midlands
Walsall: 01922 614500

Diabetes UK Northern & Yorkshire
Darlington: 01325 488606

Diabetes UK Northern Ireland
Belfast: 028 9066 6646

Diabetes UK Scotland
Glasgow: 0141 332 2700

Diabetes UK Cymru
Cardiff: 029 2066 8276

The charity for people with diabetes

10 Queen Anne Street, London W1G 9LH
Telephone 020 7323 1531 **Fax** 020 7637 3644
Email info@diabetes.org.uk **Website** www.diabetes.org.uk

Registered charity no. 215199